D1571749

Escape From Witchcraft

Six of us huddled around the table in the damp basement, staring at a single lighted candle. Slowly I intoned instructions and unrehearsed chants. The atmosphere grew blacker and a coldness filled the air, chilling my hands. Then I felt the surge of power — a sign that a supernatural force was present. Slowly I began questioning the spirit, my mind heavy in concentration.

Suddenly an overwhelming force surrounded me. I felt a venomous power about to suffocate me — an unearthly iciness swarmed and threatened me. . . . I felt damned.

Escape From Witchcraft

Roberta Blankenship

ZONDERVAN PUBLISHING HOUSE

OF THE ZONDERVAN CORPORATION
GRAND RAPIDS, MICHIGAN 49506

Escape From Witchcraft

© 1972 by The Zondervan Corporation
Grand Rapids, Michigan

Second printing March 1973
Third printing July 1973
Fourth printing October 1973

Library of Congress Catalog Card Number 72-85565

Printed in the United States of America

1785148

To Ron

*You've asked what makes me so
committed to Christ. Perhaps this
will give you the answer.
Thanks for Isaiah 66:2.*

Roberta Blankenship

Foreword

Witches are for Halloween. Or for superstitious primitives in seventeenth century Salem. That seems to be the "modern" outlook—sophisticated skepticism and a knowing smile when it comes to witchcraft.

And yet *Time's* recent cover story would indicate that witchcraft is not a thing of the past. Satan is not dead. Young people by the thousands are probing seriously the mysteries of "the other side," from seances to Satan worship. Leading universities report over-enrolled courses on witchcraft . . . occult book sales have doubled in three years . . . most American high schools have their campus "witches and warlocks" . . . and occasionally the headlines shatter our complacency with the terror of Manson-style violence.

While the drug problem occupies community attention, another epidemic—far more insidious, far more elusive—is spreading among young people. This epidemic of occult experimentation can lead from the "fun and games" of a slumber-party seance to self-destructive emotional and spiritual slavery.

But few of us comprehend the scope or seriousness of the epidemic. That is why this book had to be written.

The author is not a social theorist or scholarly theologian, but another kind of expert—*someone who has been there and back.*

The story recorded here is the *real life experience* of an American teen-ager. Roberta Blankenship, now a student at Nyack College in Nyack, New York, shares her own experiences which graphically underscore why and how modern young people get involved in the occult and the desperate searching that drives them to such dangerous answers.

Like so many, Roberta faced problems in her young life that left her feeling helpless and bitter. She reached into another world to find power to hurt, to heal, to escape.

Many "now generation" people have turned off conventional religion. They have rejected the church and God, but they have been left with a gnawing spiritual emptiness. Their spirit cries out for satisfaction, and the occult world offers a "spiritual" experience.

The "other side" can seem strangely attractive to a teen-ager faced with difficult life situations and decisions, curiosity about the future, and haunting questions about death.

It is difficult to judge the appeal or the effects of modern witchcraft from the outside. Someone must come from the inside to tell the story.

Someone has. Roberta's candid, sometimes shocking, story describes the way *into* witchcraft and what one finds there. But more important, she tells about her *escape* from witchcraft into a life of love and fulfillment.

This is much more than a story about witchcraft—it is the absorbing account of a twentieth century transformation by God's Son, Jesus Christ.

RON HUTCHCRAFT
North Jersey Director
Metropolitan Youth for Christ

Escape From Witchcraft

1

It was that dirty, puggy-nosed, freckle-faced Dorothy with one knee in a broken-down red wagon who called to me as I scuffed through the alley behind our new house on the East Side of Chicago. She called my name and waved. I recognized her face and remembered her first name. She was in my new second grade room— 201, and I soon learned that she lived across the street from us. She was 2-A and I was 2-B, which meant she was a year ahead of me at Jane Addams Elementary School. And she even knew how to write!

I was glad to have a friend, and I was glad we had moved from Hegeweisch to the East Side. Hegeweisch — with all its ugly memories. Maybe now things would be better.

Our house on the East Side had just been built, and Dorothy told me that she used to play in it before the builders had finished.

Dorothy had lost both her parents when she was about five years old. She and her two brothers were sent to live with her aunt and uncle. Her Aunt Sophie was a fat bleached blonde who always pronounced her niece's name like a harsh "Dortie." She was bossy, sloppy, and always complaining. Aunt Sophie had three boys of her own, and Dorothy confided that the only reason her aunt had taken her and her brothers after their parents' death was "the money. My aunt was real nice to us at first, but after she spent all the money she turned against us."

Personally, I thought Dorothy was lucky not to have any parents.

I didn't remember much about my real father except that he drank Budweiser but hardly ever got drunk. And I don't think he raised his voice often either. But I was only five years old when Mom divorced him. She remained single for two days and then came home with Monty, my "new" father. I didn't miss my own father, whom I thought to be just "gone," but I didn't like Monty — this new man who called me "mama's pet."

A few nights after his arrival I awoke to find Mama crouching and coughing up blood on our framed-in back porch. I had never seen anyone bleed so bad before — red, heavy clots formed under her nose like tomato paste. I was frightened. The next instant Monty was beating on the porch door, trying to break in.

My small hands shook while I dialed for the operator to help me reach the police. When Monty saw me go to the phone, he left. Mama never said a word to me — just went to clean up. That was only the beginning of the violence in our home.

And life on the East Side wasn't any easier. Mom and Monty still quarreled. Often I heard them fighting in their room. Sometimes Monty locked their door. Then I was really frightened — afraid that he would kill Mom in there and I wouldn't be able to help her. On several occasions I actually called the police, and they arrested him. When he'd get out on bail, he would bring my mother some food and try to apologize.

He's just trying to bribe her, I'd think. But at least he brought food. Food.

Mom was always busy working at Monty's Pizzeria. She usually came home at two or three in the morning and slept during the day. She was too tired to cook and hardly ever had time to go grocery shopping so the refrigerator was bare most of the time. I was ashamed to open it in front of my friends. Usually it contained only butter, milk, and a few odds and ends. My parents figured we could call the pizzeria when we were hungry and they'd send us something But greasy pizza, hamburgers, french fries, and pop were not a nutritious or satisfying diet for anyone — especially for growing children. And when the food was sent to us, we had to wait for a delivery to come to the East Side.

On the rare occasions when Mom did cook, we ate everything in sight. I told her we should have meals like that everyday and she joked, "Be glad you are getting this." There were times that we ate at two, three, or four in the morning.

I hated living like that, but I knew there was nothing I could do about it. And I was afraid to say anything for fear of being beaten. I used to leave the house or hide in my room and cover my ears so I wouldn't hear the leather slapping flesh and the cries of my brothers and sister whenever they had a "whipping" coming.

And I knew mother was helpless to do anything. Monty's constant arguing and cruelty suppressed her, and his frequent visits to the tavern two doors away from the restaurant soon had them deep in debt. Monty wasted their money on women, booze, his expensive Cadillac, and his friends — on everyone but his family.

Aunt Sophie was always whining to Dorothy, "Why can't you be neat and not gimme no sass. You stupid Dortie. Why can't you be like Roberta? I wish she was my kid." I was sure glad I wasn't. But I felt terrible whenever she threw that line at Dorothy. I didn't want Dorothy to be like me. I didn't like myself at all. And I didn't like my family.

Dorothy and I were close friends throughout grade school. We walked to school together and made up silly games as we went along. I'd ask her, "Would you play with me if I looked like this?" and I'd stick out my neck, curl my lips under to show my gums, and roll my eyes toward my nose. She'd shudder "no" as I tried to make an uglier face each time I repeated the question.

We had our own secret club — S.P.I. (Secret Persons Intelligence). We made up rules, the first being so confidential that we had to memorize it — and later forgot it. Our missions sometimes consisted of exploring abandoned cars and following people (snickering to each other and eavesdropping along the way), but most of the time we explored the rock hills near the steel mills. They were forbidden territory marked by "No Trespassing" signs which we completely ignored. Dorothy and I were sure that monsters lived within the high hills. We'd take our lunch and find a crevice among the rocks to protect us from the strong winds. We spent hours climbing over those hills, spying and exploring, always being careful not to get caught. Dorothy and I agreed that one day we were bound to witness the dumping of some poor murder victim. After all, this was Chicago.

After sixth grade, we had to transfer from Jane Addams School to Gallistel for grades seven and eight. Since Dorothy was a year ahead of me, she left when I was promoted to sixth grade. We still saw each other, but not as often. I began to wander by myself, exploring and pretending I was an archaeologist studying the Egyptian tombs and mummies. I enjoyed writing and composing pointless horror tales, poems, and songs.

I'm not sure why I was so preoccupied with horror tales. Perhaps because I lived in a world of violence — my vicious home life. Other girls enjoyed Dracula movies just as much as I did, but they also did "normal" things like having crushes on boys and reading "love" comic books, while I concentrated on writing bloody murder stories.

And I was so serious about my writing — I saved it all. Perhaps in my tales I was destroying my family. I believe Satan saw my unhappy home life, and anticipating my desire to find an outlet, he paved a way for me to find pleasure and release.

For example, in a murder story a murderer for an instant feels he has true power, and subconciously that is what I wanted. This was where Satan knew he could lead me astray — get me into the imagination of horror and then secretly interest me in the powers he later gave me.

Gradually I got into the habit of talking aloud to myself, studying aloud. Monty would say sarcastically, "She lives in a world of her own." And I did.

When the family did eat together, I often refused to sit at the table with them. I would eat alone in the basement or in my room. Sometimes Monty became angry and hit me. "You always complain about the family not eating together, and when we do, you run to a corner!"

He was right and I knew it, but I couldn't begin to explain my actions to him. I just liked being by myself so much more.

I felt no love for my family nor did I receive any from them. I didn't want their affection or their attention. When I saw Monty hurt my mom, I knew that that couldn't be love, or if it was, it was wrong. I saw love as cheap, lying, brutal, and painful. I decided that love was dirty and wanted no part of it. I heard talk about the beauty of marriage, yet I never saw any "beauty."

The ugliness of the "love" I had seen made me sick. I wanted nothing to do with my family. I just wanted to be left alone. I hated to have them touch me because I didn't want to be dishonest. I felt no affection, so why should I pretend! And during that time I never regretted these feelings I had toward my family.

My mother never asked for my affection,

mainly because she's not that type of woman. But in my young mind, I blamed Monty. I believed that all men were liars and cheats and despised them because of the example set by my stepfather.

One warm spring morning during recess Miss Foley, my sixth grade teacher, took me aside while the other kids hurried outside. Once we were alone, she asked me, "Roberta, do you mind the other girls being around you?" I looked at her rather puzzled and smiled.

"No," I answered. "I don't mind the other girls."

She began again. "What I mean, Roberta, is, do you mind being so much more mature than the other girls?"

I stared at Miss Foley and then almost laughed. "Why no. They're okay."

"And they don't bother you?"

"No. I have friends."

She explained. "Well, I thought perhaps you didn't enjoy playing with the others. You don't seem to follow along like the rest of them do."

That was true, but it was only because I was never interested in their activities and games; I found them boring.

When Miss Foley dismissed me, I went to my locker to change my books, then came back to the room and sat down. As I began reading over an assigned story, my thoughts kept wandering. *That was a strange thing for Miss Foley to ask. I never thought of that before . . . being mature. More mature. Am I really?*

2

While I was still in sixth grade, Dorothy had a birthday party in her basement one uncomfortable, humid April afternoon. Many of her friends from Gallistel were there, and Dorth had asked me to borrow some good records from my brother Curtis. We were to have lots of food, picture taking, present opening, and dancing.

Aunt Sophie took a picture of Dorth cutting her cake and then disappeared upstairs, not bothering us girls while we played unbearably loud music and danced. "The Beatles" and "The Animals" beat loudly against the cement walls.

The girls soon got bored with that scene and someone suggested, "Hey, let's have a seance." Many agreed, and someone asked who would lead it. Everyone looked at everyone else.

Suddenly I said aloud, "I will."

"Do you know how?" they asked.

"Of course I know," I quickly responded. Now I didn't even know what a seance was — had never seen one — but I told them to do exactly as I said. I didn't understand why I said what I did or how I knew what to do, but there I sat, giving instructions like a master of the black arts, ordering the girls about with some inner knowledge I never even knew had existed.

Only a few of the girls took part in the seance. The others were afraid and just watched. Somehow I knew I needed absolute silence, concentration, and obedience by the spectators as well as the participants. I gave specific instructions, repeating some of them several times. Our purpose was to contact the spirit of Dorothy's dead mother.

The seance was a success. All of us felt we had reached the unknown, unfamiliar spirit world. The girls were either thrilled or frightened. The frightened ones sensed I had a sincere power for what they had previously thought to be a game.

Personally, I felt that if we had continued longer we would have learned much more about the spirit world. But I knew that these girls weren't serious enough to continue with it, nor did they want to learn more about this new horizon which now flashed question after question into my mind. I wanted to probe it — to discover more. A strange power and strength swelled tremendously within me. This was a dimension in which I had never traveled. I had power. From where? Was it my own? Could I become stronger — more powerful? I must try. I wanted this power!

From the moment I volunteered to lead my first seance, I sensed that I had been gifted above these "ordinary" girls. And I would prove it to them.

The news of our successful seance spread through Jane Addams and Gallistel schools like fire.

"Did a spirit actually speak to you?"

"Was it really Dorothy's mother?"

"How did you know for sure?"

"Will you try again?"

Overnight I gained a new fame and popularity — a popularity I never sought. Girls anxiously planned pajama parties, spreading the word that "Roberta's leading a seance." A succession of successful seances were performed. They were so frightening that a new rage raided the blood of my female classmates.

Previously there had been hearsay about others who had tried to lead a seance, but none had been successful. Now the girls looked to me when they needed someone to satisfy their curiosity.

However, I did not take this power lightly. I believed that one had to be completely sincere when delving into the supernatural world. I prided myself on my status as a successful medium.

"Oh, please, Roberta, you're the only one who can do it right. We can't do it without you." Beg, beg, beg, until finally I gave in. For quite some time pajama parties were held every other Friday or Saturday night. If my parents ever wondered about my sudden burst of popularity, they never said anything.

Every party followed the same procedure:

1. arrival of the girls
2. refreshments, music, and dancing
3. girl talk and a gradual settling down
4. mood setters
5. seance

The mood for the seance was set by beginning

with a few "thrill-getter" games that conjured up fantasies in the girls' minds. We used popular "in-the-dark" games such as "Blue Casket" and "Mary Worth." "Mary Worth" was the real fright giver.

In "Mary Worth" the participants gather together in the dark around a mirror which has been laid flat on the center of a table or other level surface. Then the leader tells the story of Mary Worth. There are many versions, but this is the basic order: Mary Worth was a secret worshiper of the devil. One evening her husband discovered her in the midst of her Satan worship. She met death at the shock and anger of her husband. It is believed that Satan keeps her soul from rest.

"Our purpose is to bring the surviving spirit of Mary Worth before us," the leader says. Then all close their eyes and chant in unison, "I believe in Mary Worth." This is repeated until they have the nerve to open their eyes in order to catch a glimpse of Mary who has supposedly risen up from the center of the mirror.

This game causes the mind to believe in nonsense. An overactive imagination enhanced by fearful expectation could easily catch a partial reflection of any object in a room and distort the image in the dim light, causing the participants to see something frightful.

One tragic incident resulted from this game in a Chicago suburb when a young girl performed it by herself. Shock and severe fright caused her to scratch her eyes, inflicting blindness.

"Blue Casket" is another figment of the imagination. A silver fork is placed in a thin ray of light (usually from a crack in the door) within a darkened room. The participants stare at the fork until they see the formation of a coffin rise from it. Any person who is brave enough to approach the coffin and lift its lid is supposedly able to view her "chosen" mate.

Eyestrain and willing imagination enable the girls to see supernatural visages. The ray of light upon the fork refracted the beam into a smooth glow. If I used my imagination I found it easy to see a coffin, a rock, a trunk. Actually I could make the girls see whatever I thought the beam "should" be. At our parties the girls unanimously agreed that they saw a coffin.

But these were only games. The seance was the real thing — saving the "best for last."

It was always my policy to tell the girls that only I could stop the seance. I did this mainly because I thought they might become frightened and scream or leave and ruin the whole seance. If this were to happen while we were making spiritual contact, it would break the other girls' concentration and possibly cause me to lose the spirit and miss some valuable information or revelation which the spirit might offer. Also, I was the medium. I was in command of the seance.

I always used a candle in the center of the circle of participants. No other bright lights were allowed. I requested silence and told the girls to join hands. I then instructed them to concentrate on the sound of my voice and obey my words. I asked them to believe and concen-

27

trate extremely hard, never letting their thoughts travel elsewhere. I continued to encourage them as I broke off to speak to the spirit. I would state whom we wanted to see and why. Sometimes I would add a few odd chants or worship type greetings. I changed my wordage every time. It was spontaneous and unrehearsed. I spoke as I felt and believed.

Sometimes visions were seen, knocking or voices heard, objects moved about (possibly psychokinesis, which is energy transmitted by the human brain which moves objects with the mind, involving no bodily touch), scents smelled — such as tobacco when none was present.

I stopped the seance whenever I knew spiritual contact had ended. Sometimes the spirit would tell me it was leaving or the cold room would become warm or perhaps the girls would tire of concentrating (although this was rare). Of course there were times when I found it necessary to break off a seance because of insincere jokesters. I never fooled with this power — it was real. And the power was not in the ritual. It was in the sincerity of the participants.

3

Eyes followed me as I walked the halls of Gallistel as a seventh grader. I sensed my popularity, my "difference." Those who had heard of me last year now saw me in person. They asked me questions, trying to prove me a phony. They could not.

I became known as the "Edgar Allan Poe of the Seventh Grade." I had increased my writing during the free time I had in study halls, filling composition books with terror tales, their length ranging anywhere from one or two pages to approximately twenty-eight. During lunch or recess both boys and girls took my stories and sat outside, in the rest rooms, or in the classrooms to read them. My stories became so popular that I often took them along on class trips to read during the bus ride to our destination. Sometimes I read them at pajama parties to entertain the girls.

One evening we had a party at the home of one of my classmates, Barbara. Her sister, a high school senior, and one of her friends — Susan — had agreed to chaperone us.

At first we had the usual girl talk which included jokes, school happenings, boys and boyfriends, and eventually gossip about other girls whom they disliked. I was never really a part of all this, but rather observed from the sidelines. I was only there because I was useful to them. I didn't really mind though. I knew I was superior to them!

After we had eaten, a thunderstorm blew up. The atmosphere was perfect for the beginning of a seance, and all else was forgotten. We assembled in the basement and went through the preliminary games, preparing the setting, and were soon ready for "the real thing." All but five of the girls backed out. Among these five was Susan.

The six of us huddled around the table in the damp basement, staring at a single lighted candle. Susan wanted us to contact her mother who had been dead since she was twelve. Slowly I intoned instructions, warning the girls that they had to be sincere, they had to concentrate. I stressed the necessity of obeying my instructions — a type of formula where one had to react, not act.

The atmosphere grew blacker and a coldness filled the air, chilling my hands. Then I felt the surge of power — a sign that a supernatural force was present. I felt ready to delve into the unknown again and began questioning the spirit. Things ran smoothly, calmly, my mind heavy in concentration. Suddenly an overwhelming force surrounded me. For the first time in my experience I felt a venomous power about to suffocate me. "It will harm us," I thought. An unearthly iciness swarmed and threatened me.

"Break it off!" I called to stop the seance.

"Break it off quick! Hurry up. Turn on the lights!"

But before anyone could move, Susan pleaded, "Mother, if you are here, give me a sign."

Suddenly the window above the table where we were seated burst open and a flesh-colored image with human female features hovered across the darkened room near the ceiling above our heads to the left of the group. It moved quite rapidly with a diminishing tail of ghostly flesh trailing after it.

Then havoc broke loose and the lights came on. The girls ran upstairs — away. Away from what? From me? From the spirit? From fear? Why had I felt something evil present as I never had before? I sat wondering if my powers had been challenged.

A girl scurried down the stairway to me. "Hurry, Roberta. Go upstairs!" I heard commotion as I rushed up the stairs and into the living room. The girls were gathered around Susan, who was sitting on the couch in hysterics — crying, screaming. The moment she saw me, she pointed and screamed threateningly, "Get out! I hate you. Get away from me. I never want to see you again. Go away!"

I said nothing but went back to the basement. I kept seeing her face, her pointing finger. Kept hearing, "I hate you."

Apparently Susan hadn't believed that the spirit world could be reached. I felt that she should be grateful, but the shock of *the reality of the supernatural* had frightened her.

Later Barbara told me that Susan had been

taken home, and I never heard from nor saw her again. The spirit face had not smiled, and Susan had never acknowledged that the image was the face of her mother. Others said it was. Having never seen her mother, I had to accept their word for it.

Needless to say, no more seances were performed that evening. Throughout the night I listened to the comments and chatter of the other girls; they had received the thrill they sought, and I anticipated the news that would run through the school on Monday. Wearily I laid in my blankets on the floor. Outside I could hear the whistle of an oncoming train. As it passed the house, vibrations caused a glass to fall and shatter in front of my face.

Had the devil done that? Had that been the venomous spirit present tonight? I felt damned.

But this was only the beginning.

4

I found myself writing more — alone more. In my solitude I heard the others whispering "witch" behind my back. From their expressions, I knew their whispered conversations were about me. In my own paranoid way I began to desire revenge — revenge upon these two-faced enemies. I developed a strong hatred for many acquaintances.

"I can overpower them. I know I can," I constantly told myself. I determined to rise above everyone and scare away the vision which haunted my mind — the vision of Susan's pointing fingers and horrid crying. I determined to master the forces I encountered through the seances.

I began an in-depth study of the spirit world through intensive reading. Within the boundaries of my body lay an unquenchable power waiting to be released — power of soul and mind. I wanted to develop that power for my own benefit. I wanted to be superior to those around me.

I began to have some psychic experiences. During Robert Kennedy's campaign for the presidency, I had a nightmare of premonition. In the dream I was seated in a park and I saw a black car pass with an extended arm firing a gun at me but hitting Kennedy. Once hit, he fell in my arms, the blood from a wound near the base of his skull covered my hands. I awoke crying.

"I know it sounds a lot like John Kennedy's assassination," I confided to a classmate, "but even though it won't happen exactly that way, I know it's going to happen. Remember my words."

Three days later Robert Kennedy was killed. I didn't know what to think. Was it really a premonition about Kennedy or did it actually apply to me in some way? Was it the supernatural? Weird superstition? I knew I must seek more answers. I must know if there were powers to harness.

I began to spend the majority of my time learning to improve my powers, and the psychic experiences became more frequent and accurate. I learned to concentrate, to think as another person did and attempt to foretell his thoughts and actions. It was wonderful to "see through" people, discover their weaknesses and expose them. I hated big-shot pretenders, braggarts, and phonies.

In seventh grade I became friends with a girl named Josie. She had moved to the East Side from the Chicago suburb of Riverdale. Her family lived in a house just a few doors from us. At first Josie didn't pay much attention to my jabberings about "unseen beings," but she confessed that she thought I was a little smarter and deeper than any other person she had met. As our friendship developed, our discussions went into more depth. Time after time we talked late into the night about the cloud of powerful mystery surrounding my life. We made several attempts to analyze each other.

"I always have dreams that I will die and go to hell," Josie said. "I see the devil in my dreams trying to grab me." She assured me, though, that she loved and believed in God. Several times she said, "I don't understand why you're supposed to fear God . . . if He loves you."

Josie's family was Catholic. Her mother kept a small altar in their den. Some of the statues were very old. Near it was an old ink sketch of a praying Virgin Mary. Josie told me that the picture once came to life for her grandmother, as her grandmother was a highly religious woman. "Almost a saint" Josie often said. Her ill grandmother had claimed the picture came to life telling her something about the life of Josie's father. I thought her illness had caused the woman to hallucinate, but I never told Josie that. I knew it would only create an argument or bad feelings. 1785148

Josie and I enjoyed spending the night at each other's homes. She had a small wall plaque of the heart of Christ with thorns wrapped around it. She told me that at night she would stare at the heart through the blackness and see it glow. I marveled when she said she saw the heart swell, pump, and bleed, but I could never look at that heart when I stayed there at night.

Josie's mother, Mrs. Vee, had some psychic powers and was a student of astrology. She made the astrological charts of all her children. Once finished, she told me she'd be delighted to do mine. My chart showed the break-up of my family and a rough childhood. I was assured of success and a natural death at a ripe old age.

"*Too common,*" I thought. I became a critic of astrology buffs. Horoscopes in magazines were foolishness. I was furious at people who made money by producing nothing more than logic and common sense. Example: "Good day . . . especially for business. Attack all offers with caution and consideration." I felt that people just looked to these meaningless words to gain some self-confidence. People who were admitting they were weak, thinking that gaseous stars which have no heart, mind, or soul could understand or control the human heart, mind, and soul.

"*I'm no fool,*" I thought. Half the writers of such columns paid little attention to actually "charting the stars." True, some did, such as Mrs. Vee and her friends, but they still said nothing that common sense couldn't tell you. The trick was to make a "universal appeal."

Soon, through the instruction of Mrs. Vee, I was learning the arts of palmistry, tarot and tea leaf reading, usage of the crystal ball (I borrowed hers to practice with), hypnotism, and handwriting analysis. Mrs. Vee only *introduced* these crafts to me. I continued furthering my development, soon exceeding her abilities — exceeding them so much that soon I did readings for her, her family, and her friends. Many, many times when I was visiting Josie, Mrs. Vee would talk with me. Often she smiled and said, "You are definitely psychic. Many people are, but

36

your powers are great. It's written all over your face. There's no doubt about it. You are psychic."

I took great pride in my knowledge of these crafts and in my high degree of accuracy. I began reading tarot cards and palms for many people. I felt confident and natural in these readings and soon found that the success in these crafts did lie within myself. When I took a person's hand in my own or laid out the cards, I instantly was able to give accurate information about a person I had never met before.

In a couple of cases I could barely tell a thing, and I knew the person had to be a disbeliever or doubter. When I encountered people like this, I immediately "felt" it and told them what I sensed. They left knowing they couldn't fool me. They were dealing with a person who had true contact with the spirit world and the power of the supernatural.

I developed powers of levitation to a minor degree and could move small objects such as books or coat hangers without touching them. I never used these powers extensively, mainly because I found them unnecessary and not usable enough to be effective and *challenging*. I was satisfied with the knowledge that it could be done and that I could do it.

5

One thing which amazes me as I look back at that period of my life is that neither my mother nor stepfather *ever* questioned my activities away from home. To my parents, pajama parties were just that — pajama parties. They had no idea of my interest in or growing involvement with the occult world.

I brought home good grades and reports. Teachers commented on my excellent classroom conduct and polite, respectful attitude. As long as this continued, which it did, my parents never questioned me, apparently confident that my after-school life was the same.

My mom never praised me much or said anything about my good school record and behavior, and this rather bothered me. I wanted her to be proud of me. I never stole, smoked, swore, fought, or caused trouble as my sister and brothers did. Because of this, I felt growing resentment toward my brothers and sister. I guess I really did want my parents' attention, but not the kind they gave me. I suppose they had a sort of trust in me which I didn't appreciate, although I was grateful they didn't badger and question me about what I did in my spare time or with my friends. I didn't want them in my business. At times I wanted them to know about my extraordinary powers, but I never told them. If they had ever found out and tried to interfere, I don't know what I would have done in desperation.

6

"Witch . . . witch . . . witch," the words echoed in my mind every time I saw the kids at school. Little cliques standing in groups whispering. "Roberta . . . she's some kinda witch." I knew it wasn't my imagination because several girls came to me and told me the names of the girls who were the whisperers. They wanted to know why I was different, and gradually I became nonchalant about the whole thing — not caring what others said. I had power! Even my friends were becoming afraid of me.

I wrote to an international witch organization which sent me newsletters containing the latest happenings among witches, warlocks, astrologers, and other branches of the clan throughout the world. The letters had listings of warehouses where one could buy the equipment, books, herbs, and other things needed to perform various rituals and incantations.

Soon I became disgusted however. Under my breath I chanted, "The power lies in the self and *not* in devices."

Generally a coven is a gathering of thirteen people who claim spiritual powers. Covens categorize the females as witches and the males as warlocks. These small groups gather to unite their powers to strengthen themselves.

The international organization sent a form

from a particular group which wanted to know if I would like to join one of the four covens listed. I noticed that the last one was "Satanic" — supposedly the strongest of the four. There were more sects of covens than were on this list, but these four were supposed to be the "top-notchers." They said they would contact a coven in Chicago if I were to give my consent.

The purpose of the questionnaire was to "classify" my powers to see if I would qualify or meet their standards for membership. As I read the form I became enraged.

"Classify *me* to see if I qualify for them! Who do they think they are?" I was furious. I didn't need them. I saw them as weak, without faith in their own powers, needing others to bolster them. "I don't need them!" I shouted, ripping up the papers and throwing them away. I wrote to them telling how foolish and weak I thought they were.

These newsletters had also contained listings of witches or warlocks who desired to correspond with others of their kind — pen pals, so to speak. At one time I did consider the idea, but finally decided against it. I was satisfied with the greatness of my own powers and did not want to share them with anyone.

Because of my increased powers I found myself in great demand. Girls and boys, men and women approached me for palm readings. One Saturday in the Loop I noticed an elderly woman behind a display of astrology books in Woolworth's Department Store. I listened as she gave her sales pitch to all who stopped to thumb through the books. I struck up a conversation with her, and she told me she had been an actress. I then told her of my powers. I read her palm and amazed her when I accurately told her of the son she had lost, her stillborn baby, and the husband who had deserted her. While I did this, observers began to gather around. Soon there was a line of people wanting to have their palms read.

A black nurse took my address, asking if I would advise her on certain business problems if she wrote to me. I must admit I did feel rather silly standing in that dime store with a line of people anxious to see what the young "witch" had to tell them. I didn't like being the center of attention in that way.

Another time in the Loop area a man handed me a card advertising a female seeress on the southeast side of Chicago. Laughing, I threw it away. I didn't need her power, nor would I put money in the pocket of a probable member of the expanding ring of so-called mediums who ninety percent of the time were just good actors and actresses.

One evening Josie, two of her sisters, and myself held a seance in Josie's bedroom. I was aware that Josie's older sister had doubts about my abilities, but she was curious and wanted to be in on it. The purpose that evening was to make contact with an uncle of their family. During the course of the seance, I experienced my first trance in which the spirit actually took control over my speech to communicate with the other participants. When it was finished I was

43

exhausted and had no recollection of what I had said. Josie and her sisters excitedly told me all they had witnessed. They said I had spoken in a different voice — not my own — and when I stopped I laid my head on the table, staying in that position for so long they feared I might be dead.

Meanwhile, life at home was still horrible. Our house was permeated with the vile odors of smoke and alcohol. Dirty magazines lay strewn about — no food — a dirty house. I tried to help when I could, but Mom was either working or tired and upset from searching for Monty who seemed always sick or drunk somewhere. I hated liquor and what it had made of my stepfather.

Whenever an argument began, I left the house. Many times in the dead of the night I felt like a helpless prisoner forced to listen to Mom scream and cry, to watch Monty choke and punch her — to watch the clawing, throwing, beating as they battled with each other.

When my younger brother Perry and I were left home alone — which often happened — I stayed awake during the darkest hours wanting to be alert if a burglar should try to break in. Mom kept a lock on the phone so the bill wouldn't be so large, and I imagined myself trying to break that lock off to call for help.

On weekends Monty usually stumbled home on Sunday morning drunk and vomiting. Later one of us would have to clean up after him. Disease infected his legs so that they swelled until the veins broke. Doctors warned him to stay away from the alcohol. He would try for a week or so, but it never lasted. Many times Perry or I would have to stay home to boil towels in water and boric acid and then wrap them around his legs. Day after day we worked to heal those legs, but to no avail. The alcohol and Monty's excess weight won the battle.

Since the majority of my stepfather's friends were alcoholics or drunks, I began to believe that almost every family must be exposed to this life style of booze and battle. No one I knew seemed happy. Taxes and bills went unpaid. All of us kids were left with instructions not to tell anyone where Monty worked or what his business phone number was or if he was home, for fear the caller might be a bill collector.

They are all weak, I thought. *My father should be wiser because he is older, but he is not. I am.* I tried to shut out the continuous arguing and noise, but the voices rang too loudly.

7

Many people who crossed me found themselves victims of my vicious temper and my powers — often unknowingly.

When I was in the sixth grade a girl named Debbie had a part in our class play. Tall and slender, Debbie was supposed to dance with a boy about three times larger than she. Debbie had heard about some of the things I did at the parties and jokingly requested that I make her partner sick with a fever so she wouldn't have to dance with him.

The afternoon of the play as I watched Debbie dance with the stand-in, I had visions of her original partner who was home suffering with the mild fever I had put on him.

After the play I asked Debbie if she had enjoyed her stand-in partner. She gave me a strange look, realizing that I had actually done what she asked. From that time on she never spoke much to me and gave me the feeling of "witch" every time she saw me.

I never caused the death of a person through my hexes and powers, but the temptation often presented itself.

The only "curse" I ever cast on any member of my family was directed against my youngest stepbrother Monfre. When he was around we argued continually. He taunted me constantly, calling me "witch." One day in a cruel, half-crazed moment I mocked, "You better run. I'm a vampire!" I bit down on his arm brutally until it bled.

My stepfather was furious. "Why did you tell him you are a vampire? Are you crazy? If he goes home and his mother sees his arm like that, she could take me to court and sue us for every penny I've got! Why are you like this? When are you two gonna stop fighting? I ought to beat both of you." I ran out of the house as Monty kept shouting over and over, "She's crazy . . . she's crazy."

I walked down the alley and out to the rock hills by the steel mills. I climbed up on the rock mounds which had so often lured me and found a crevice in which to hide.

Can I really be losing my mind, I wondered.

"No, you're not," a voice whispered. "They want you to think you are, but you're not. You're strong, powerful. Don't let them step on you."

My stepbrother is my enemy. I don't need him. I hate him. He had caused me to receive a scolding; he had run and tattled like a baby. I wanted him to fail. Then I could laugh down at him and he'd know I was superior. Making sure that I was quite alone, I called for my powers and cursed him. I asked that his school grades would drop and that eventually he would drop out of high school and become a trouble-some pest to all he encountered. I wanted to see his future collapse.

When I arrived back home, Monty had gone and Monfre approached me.

48

"You know Dad's right," he began. "If I had to go to court and the judge asked me if I thought you were mean enough to use a knife, I would say yes. And I'd say it on a Bible."

"I don't want to talk about it," I replied. "Don't start another argument with me."

"I'm not trying to," he said. "But if my mother sees this on my arm, I'll tell her the truth. If we went to court they could put you away. My mother would think you're crazy."

I sensed myself beginning to boil again, so I begged him to stop bothering me. For the next few days Monfre made remarks about the bite, teasing me about being a vampire. I wished the whole thing had never occurred, but secretly I knew he would pay.

8

I continued my study of astrology and also began to consider trying my powers as a hypnotist. I wrote to various places for information, but the only sense I could derive from the material was that it was another moneymaking gimmick. The trick of hypnosis seemed to be the mastery of mind over matter using a weak or willing subject. I decided that I would demonstrate it at the next pajama party. I did, and on my first attempt successfully hypnotized a willing subject. I found the whole thing rather boring, however, and never bothered with it again.

At several of the recent parties the girls had been consulting Ouija boards. Some of the more skeptical ones said they felt it was the vibrations from their hands which moved the disc. I told them to let the powers move the disc and leave their hands off. I had received my own board from my parents who thought it was just another game.

One Sunday morning I woke to hear the bedroom radio blasting away. As I lay there, my mind tuned in to the program. WLS was reporting on occultism, and a woman on the program claimed that she had used Ouija boards. She said that when she had asked the board where the messages came from, the disc had spelled out either d-e-v-i-l or s-a-t-a-n. I had only caught the last few minutes of the show, but the young woman's words had stimulated my interest and I wanted to know more. I listened to WLS the following Sunday morning, but the show covered a different topic.

Perhaps the devil does have some influence over the Ouija board, I began to think.

Not long after that, I sat straight up in bed one night. My hands were flat on the mattress supporting myself as I looked into what appeared to be total grayness. The atmosphere was extremely warm and I was not afraid. From behind me came a gentle masculine voice which sounded as if it were directed to my right ear. It instructed me to stop performing seances. "Never lead a seance again — permanently." The voice warned that if I did. . . . I never recalled what else it had said, but I knew I must obey and I felt that I should tell no one about it. I stared into the blackness of my room. Had I dreamt it? No. It seemed too real. But even if it had been only a dream, I felt it was an angel speaking to me.

I lay in bed wide awake and I spoke these words aloud. "God, I don't know why, but I believe You do exist. I know I'm destined for hell, but even if You never know it, I'll always love You in my heart and I don't know why." My words haunted me. "I'll always love You in my heart and I *don't know why.*" I had never said that before. How could I let God know I cared about Him? Had it been just a dream?

Was it a heavenly contact? Or was I crazy? I was beginning to think so.

I started hearing voices in my head and chanting mixed with laughter — voices which told me what I should do. I had never heard these voices before, and I was worried. They badgered me constantly. I refused to admit to myself that I was losing my sanity. I tried to keep every petty thing out of my mind.

"*I* must have control, no one else," I kept telling myself.

The family problems grew — the arguing and senseless brutality. The girls who had once called me "friend" turned their backs on me when I refused to perform any more seances. "Why? Why?" they asked, searching for reasons. Did my parents forbid me? A relative? Did the devil scare me?

I couldn't tell them. Not now. When I quit leading seances, the pajama parties didn't stop, but I was no longer invited. Girls came up to me and begged me to lead, but I stood firm. I could not and would not. I heard several accounts of other girls attempting to lead the seances, but they were all failures or frauds.

"It's not the same unless you're there to make it work," a girl said. But my decision was final. And so was theirs.

I woke up and took a good look at who my friends were. *Two-faced users,* I thought. The more I dwelt on it, the more my hatred grew. I wanted revenge. They would pay. They could not do this to me — not to someone with powers such as I had mastered.

9

One night when both my parents were at work and my sister and brothers had gone somewhere, I was home alone. I sat in my room with the door shut and the lights out. Crouched on the bed, I examined the forces against me. I hated being with my family. I had lost interest in any form of friendship since the ones I had called "friends" had treated me the way they had.

Soon I would begin my freshman year at George Washington High School and I loathed the idea of having to meet new people — having to act friendly when in my heart I hated everyone. Perhaps running away would be the answer. But what would it prove?

I had become a nervous, highly emotional person. Before, I rarely cried or smiled. Now I cried at the slightest thing. *What am I going to do?* I thought desperately. *What am I doing?* A person with my powers should know, but I didn't. I was tired, so tired. I couldn't stand to listen to my family anymore. Why did they have to keep complaining and fighting? Why didn't they stop? How could I escape?

"Give me an answer, someone!"

It wasn't long before I began to think about suicide. I visualized my parents at my funeral — my mother crying. I wanted them all to cry.

Suicide. It seemed so easy. I could make it quick. Running in front of a car would do it. Twice I tried, but both times the cars screeched to a stop, the drivers cursing and screaming at me.

The voice in my head continued. "You know that you're wasting time. Are you afraid? You're foolish if you don't carry out what you're thinking." I didn't need to ask myself if I was afraid. I knew I had lost my sanity.

A few nights later Josie came over to our house looking for something to do. Since it was a quiet, warm evening and curfew not until eleven, we decided to go swinging at Wolfe Park. The park lay about a block away on Mackinaw Avenue and the grounds were brightened at night by a few lights.

Pleased to find no one else there when we arrived, I ran up to the park house fountain for a drink while Josie stayed at the swings. I was hidden from view by the building. Suddenly Josie walked over to me and whispered, "I just saw some guy who kept staring at me. I think he's drunk." There was a gate nearby, but we headed through a broken section of the fence which was closer.

The guy was waiting there! He grabbed my arm and just missed hitting my head with a heavy object. I screamed and he pushed me up against a tree and began choking me, making vicious grunting noises. Josie stood frozen with fear while I screamed and struggled and pleaded for help. Somehow I gouged my teeth into his hand and got a mouthful of blood. He broke his grip, and Josie and I fled to a friend's house across from the park and her father drove us home. I was afraid to tell my parents the whole thing, but when I mentioned that a drunk had chased us, they laughed about it.

The next morning when I was home by myself I brooded about the incident. "Why did this happen to me . . . me of all people . . . with powers like mine? If that man knew what I could do, he would have been afraid to abuse me, afraid to touch me. He will pay! He will pay!"

I called Josie and told her that I planned to put a hex on him. I returned to the park to look for anything which might belong to him. I found a carton of cigarettes and the brick with which he had tried to hit me. Then I went home to prepare and perform the incantation.

I dressed myself in black, cursing like a mad woman. "He will die for that. I'll destroy him. He'll suck the wrath of hell!" I ran around the house chanting, "Give me power. Draw it up out of my soul from the very roots of hell."

Suddenly I fell on my knees. Realization poured over me. The powers that I had thought were my own gifts were really the devious tricks of the devil. Tricks used to trap me. My powers were produced by and rooted in evil. For almost three years I had blindly claimed these powers as my own, never realizing whose puppet I had become.

The sound of thunder echoed within the walls of my mind and a voice crackled, "You stupid fool. Where did you think you got your power from?" It laughed. "Not yourself." And laughed again. "I'm not through with you."

I screamed aloud, hoping I could hear my own voice above the other. "I'm crazy. I'm crazy. Kill me, I'm crazy." I ran to the kitchen and grabbed a butcher knife, ready to slash my wrists.

Suddenly I froze as the voice continued, "I'm not through with you. You've just begun. So do as I say." And the next thing I knew, I, Roberta Blankenship, bowed down on my knees, raised my arms into the air, and said, "Satan, you are my master and prince. I know you are my source of power. Use me as you will. I am yours."

With that I fell flat on the floor and cried, "The devil is real."

10

"Millions of grains of sand in the world, why such a lonely beach?"

The bed covers were insulating me uncomfortably on such a beautiful summer evening. "I'm alone," whispered a voice. "It would be nice to have someone to talk to, someone to understand me." But no one would understand me.

"Lie there, Roberta, and feel sorry for yourself. You found out what people are. Trust them and they knife you in the back. Are you still thinking of the possibility of true friendship? Don't kid yourself. Even your closest friend Dorothy has doubts about you. Who can you trust? Even your great powers seem to be unable to bring you companionship. Is that what you want?"

I got so tired of listening to those voices. Was it because I was hearing the truth? How could I stop them? I couldn't. "Where is a voice to answer mine? I'm all alone in the world."

September came and with it my freshman year. During the early part of the fall I made a few friends, and met some girls who claimed to be "white" or "black" witches. Occasionally girls who had never known me before would approach me and ask if what they'd heard about the seances was true. I'd end up reading tarot cards or palms for them or giving psychic advice. Whatever the need, I applied my talents. I felt like a freak.

Questions still arose about why I had stopped leading seances. Finally I just had to tell Dorothy — I couldn't lie to her. When other girls asked me, I told them I had been forbidden, but I never told them by whom. But I had known Dorothy for so long, and she had been my first friend on the East Side — my closest friend. I wanted to trust her so I told her about my vision, hoping she'd believe me. She did. And she told me she thought I was right to obey the "voice" of God through a heavenly medium. Later I also told Josie who wondered if it seemed believable.

But the devil's demons were always there. At night I often felt the presence of evil around me. I could hear the laughter in my head. I thought I saw phantom shadows with sickly smiles. Voices called from deep within me. I imagined an early death for myself since I had lost the desire to live. In fact, my hopes rested on the gift of an early death, for Satan would not allow me to die by my own hand. He had a plan for me.

I learned that there were no people with special powers of their own to reach the supernatural. They were all weak people who drew from an unknown source of power, admitting they were not satisfied with their lives. Weak people who drew from resources more powerful than earth's gravity — Satan's resources.

I wished that I could stop everything. I was so tired. Satan used my weakness against me.

He tried to frighten me deeper into his keeping.

Often I lay awake aching with loneliness, talking to myself and crying. This loneliness was almost the worst impact of all. And sometimes at night I would hear my quiet voice saying, "I'll always love You in my heart and I don't know why."

11

During my freshman year I had two periods of chorus. One was girls' chorus and the other was mixed chorus. I dropped my study hall to take both of these. I thought it might be helpful to me if I could get into some clubs or activities.

Josie had a crush on a junior named Dave Zimney who was president of the high school Youth for Christ (YFC) group. She was anxious to go to one of their meetings, hoping she might really get acquainted with Dave. So one Tuesday in November we both went to their meeting which began at seven o'clock in the high school auditorium. Neither of us knew what to expect since we had never been to anything like this. We dressed casually in shirts and jeans.

Most of the meeting consisted of games and lots of laughter and goofing off. I got duped into being a guinea pig for a game of "Hairdresser" where my partner tied fresh lettuce and carrots in my hair. We won the prize, but it looked like my hair would never be the same again. Josie and I enjoyed the fun — and it was certainly what I needed.

Near the end of the evening an extremely attractive young man, Mike Aemmer, was introduced as the guest speaker. He began talking about Jesus Christ and what He could mean to us. He spoke briefly and to the point. Each sentence seemed well thought out and concise. I was very impressed with him and what he said. While our heads were bowed waiting for a closing prayer, I listened as Mike spoke of hell.

"You think you're gonna go to hell and have a big beer party with all the gang, but you're wrong. You won't have anyone." The words really hit me, and my heart began pounding. I was getting warm and wanted to leave. I knew that hell was my destination.

After the prayer, Josie and I looked at each other with tears in our eyes.

Before we left, we filled out a little blue slip of paper which I figured was for the club record since Jo and I were new members. As we walked down Avenue O, we talked about Mike and what a good speaker he was.

Josie said, "I know I'm going to hell."

"Me too," I replied. It wasn't a very happy scene — two girls walking down the street looking forward to an eternity in hell.

Two days later when I rushed into the house at four o'clock, the phone was ringing. It was the student YFC secretary and she said a YFC counselor would like to make an appointment to speak with me. I couldn't imagine why, but I consented. One afternoon a few days later the secretary met me after school and led me to the counselor's car.

Ron Hutchcraft, Southeast Area YFC Director, didn't know what he was getting into when I plopped in his car that afternoon and introduced myself. He asked me what had interested me most when I listened to the message at the YFC meeting. I didn't understand what he was trying to get at so I made up a line.

"Oh, something he said about God."

Ron took it from there and began to draw me out. He was so serious and sincere that I knew I could level with him. I began to ask questions and was impressed by his knowledge of the Bible and by the way he used Scripture to answer my questions — questions no one else had even tried to answer.

I told Ron everything about me and my imprisonment in the satanic world of the occult. I wasn't sure he would even believe me, but he did. I also told him that I knew I was destined for hell.

Three and a half hours later a miracle had occurred. I emerged from Ron's car a "new" person. I had accepted Jesus Christ as my Savior and Redeemer. Jesus would not look back on the horrible things I had done. He had forgiven me and I was free! Free from the chains of Satan!

Someone really loves me, was my first thought. *I can feel it. I love you, Jesus. Please keep me.*

I'll never forget that most glorious day in my life. I was free from Satan! I was through with the devil.

But the devil was not through with me!

12

Ron Hutchcraft warned me that the devil would do his best to upset me. He was right. That first wonderful night of Christianity brought me running in the door shouting joyfully, "Mom, I'm going to heaven! I'm saved!"

My mother just looked at me. "What?"

"I've accepted Jesus as my Savior."

"You'll get over it," she replied rather haughtily. "I was that way when I was your age too. It'll wear off."

"No it won't. This is real to me."

Mom's lack of enthusiasm stunned me and I went to my room with tears in my eyes. My brothers began to tease me by sarcastically referring to me as "Christian."

My life had only begun that chilly November day when I discovered the love of Christ. With Jesus in my life my attitude toward my family changed immensely. I wanted to help my stepfather with his drinking problem. I also wanted to make amends with my stepbrother Monfre. I was sorry about the horrible curse I had cast on him. I asked God to forgive me and to help Monfre.

But it seemed that the family troubles doubled. My mother argued that nobody knew whether or not they would go to heaven. She said many people believed that we already had hell right here on earth, that God had abandoned us. I knew she was wrong, but it was no use arguing about it. My brothers would join in and say that I prctended to be an "angel," but that I would suffer in hell with them.

The teasing persisted and I prayed that it would stop. I was afraid my temper would snap. My nerves became shakier and shakier. I often cried alone in my room, spiritually wrapped in the arms of God, "You are all I have, Jesus."

I wanted my family to know that Jesus could end the strife we had, but they wouldn't listen. It hurt me when I thought of myself in heaven and the others in hell. But none of them understood. My brothers kept telling me it was all in my head.

I must have faith to become strong, I thought. I realized that prayer and patience must be my partners in my hope that one day Jesus could claim my family as a part of His.

I tried to maintain good Bible study habits. I wanted to learn as much as I could. I asked Ron scores of questions, and he never disappointed me because the answers existed — all of them from the Bible.

Late one evening the phone rang and someone hollered for me to answer it.

"It's Ron Hutchcraft," I whispered to my stepbrother Joe.

He snickered back, "It's her boyfriend, Hunchback."

68

"Don't say things like that," I scolded with my hand over the receiver. "He's a married man." But his laughter continued.

Ron had called to tell me about the YFC International Convention which was to be held that year in Chicago. He wanted me to testify at a banquet to be held at the Sheraton-Chicago Hotel just off Michigan Avenue in the Loop area.

Just the thought of speaking before a large crowd like that thrilled me. I would have an opportunity to tell others about this love of Christ for me — tell them about the miracle He had done in my life.

"Hold the line a minute, Ron. I'll check with my folks."

Mom and Monty were in bed watching television when I ran in to tell them the exciting news.

"Guess where I get to go!"

"Where?" Monty asked.

"To speak at a YFC banquet in the ballroom of the Sheraton-Chicago downtown."

"How are you gonna get there?" Mom asked.

"Someone from YFC will take me," I answered. "Can I go?"

"I don't know," Monty replied.

I began to get frantic. "Ron's waiting on the phone for an answer."

Monty became angry. "I don't care who's on the phone. I don't know."

Fear filled my heart. "I've just got to go."

"You're not going anywhere unless we say so," Monty shouted.

69

I began to cry. "You can't stop me. I'm going for Jesus."

"Over my dead body you are," Monty raved. "You tell whoever Ron Hutchcraft is that you're staying here."

I ran to the phone, crying as I told Ron I couldn't go. He said not to get upset and that he would talk with me about it again in a few days. When I hung up even my stepbrother Joe felt sorry for me.

"Aw, don't cry. Dad'll let you go."

"No he won't," I sobbed.

"Yes he will," Joe reassured. "You shouldn't of got so excited and raised your voice."

"I couldn't help it. It's so important to me."

"Dad knows it," Joe said. "He'll let you go. Just be quiet. You'll only make him mad if you don't."

The following week when Ron called again I could tell him that my parents had consented to my going. I was happy that it was finally settled. This opportunity really meant so much to me. I wanted to find a way to let others know what Christ had done for me — how He changed my life — and now He had provided a way.

At the banquet that night Ron asked me a couple of questions that I could answer in detail and yet not take a great deal of time. Later many people came to me and said they were amazed at the acid taste of life I had gotten at such an early age. They knew many kids who had family and emotional problems, but they weren't aware that some in their insecurity and trouble might turn to witchcraft, astrology, and even worshiping Satan. I realized that this might be a special ministry for me since I knew more and more high school kids were getting mixed up in occultism.

I began attending the YFC rallies which were held at the Moody Memorial Church in Chicago. The church seated approximately 7,000 people, although not that many kids came to every rally.

I enjoyed walking through Moody Church with its massive halls and stairways — old and powerful. Hundreds of huge organ pipes soared to the ceiling, and I could imagine the heavy music echoing through the halls. I loved that church. Somehow I felt especially close to God there.

13

Summer came all too quickly bringing its overwhelming boredom. Satan attacked my thoughts, making me extremely temperamental. The P.T.A. had given me a choral scholarship for eight lessons. I went downtown once a week, feeling sorry for poor Mr. Scanlan, my instructor. I'm sure he never did believe I was a Christian from the way I treated him. I hated the awful music I had to learn. I wanted to study jazz. So, I wasted my eight lessons. In fact, I wasted my entire vacation eating and sitting around watching television day and night.

In the fall, my sophmore year, a friend from school who enjoyed YFC activities mentioned that she was planning to audition for a YFC-sponsored group called "The Voices of Teen-Age Chicago." That sounded good to me and I considered trying too. I talked to Dave Zimney about it, and he encouraged me to "at least try" and offered to give me a ride to the hall where the auditions would be held.

But that Saturday morning I chickened out. I hid in the basement while my brother Perry told Dave to go on without me since I wasn't ready. Instead, Dave said he'd be back again for me in a half hour, so I had no excuse. I was ready when he returned.

When we arrived at the hall, I was amazed

at the number of teens who had shown up for the audition. Some of them had fantastic voices — I knew I'd never make it. Then came another shock. The auditions were on an individual basis — and I didn't know how to read music. Oh how I wished I had listened to Mr. Scanlan and what he had so patiently tried to teach me.

When it was my turn, I went into a little room where two men were sitting. One was the director, Gene Mastin. I explained to him that I couldn't read music, and he had me sing "America, the Beautiful." When I had finished, he handed me a songbook. "Sing that," he said.

"But I can't read music. I don't know this song."

"I know," he smiled.

The pianist began and I stumbled through the song, praying all the way.

"Okay, start over again," he said.

I made another nervous attempt with a slight improvement.

When I finished, Gene asked me why I wanted to be in the group.

"I want to sing about Jesus and how much I love Him. I've heard your group at some of the rallies and I like your style of music." That was it. I left the room in a cold sweat, certain that I had blown it.

Two weeks later I got my acceptance letter. I was in! I couldn't believe it!

Besides singing at rallies, "Voices" did concerts at churches, naval bases, shopping plazas, and banquets. That year the group performed at the YFC Fall Banquet which was held at the

Sheraton-Chicago and Ron called me out to give my testimony.

Afterwards people came up to me, some just saying, "Praise the Lord," while others wanted to talk. One young couple said, "We wanted to ask you if following horoscopes is a pretty bad thing? We read ours all the time." They assured me they had been Christians for a long time.

"I can only speak for myself," I said, "but horoscopes and astrology are bad if you live your life by them. I know I couldn't. I have more faith in Jesus than to go to such extremes. Plus, if we believe in the Lord, we don't need that kind of crutch for reassurance. There are too many who read the horoscopes more than the Bible." They seemed satisfied with my answer.

"You know," the young woman said, "it's so hard to imagine you doing the things you say you did." I just smiled. I wished I had some biblical references to give them to support my statements and beliefs, and I decided then that I needed to do more intense Bible research and study. If I continued my public witnessing many people would be approaching me with questions and I needed to be prepared.

Soon I had a busy schedule of speaking engagements. One afternoon I got excused early from school to travel to Wheaton, Illinois, where I had been invited to speak to a group of sixth and eighth graders. The children were attentive and responsive. It didn't surprise me to see that the majority of them had already been participating in seances. As usual, I ran overtime trying to answer all their questions. When the children were being dismissed for the day, the puzzled glance of a dark-haired boy caught my attention. Sensing he had a problem, I asked him to come over to me.

"What have you got to do with all this?" I asked him.

He smiled. "I practice voodoo."

"How much?" I asked.

"I believe in poking pins in dolls. I know it works."

"Have you ever hurt anybody? It's a very dangerous game. Don't you realize that the devil is the source of your power? He'll harm you. Get out of it."

He was interested, but the teacher was calling him. "Can I write to you?" he asked.

"Of course." I gave him my address but he never wrote.

From my speaking engagements at women's clubs, I learned that many mothers were worried because they knew their daughters had Ouija boards or went to pajama parties where seances were held.

"What can I do?" inquired one youthful looking mother. "Should I take her board away or forbid her to go to the seances or what?"

"No," I said. "Don't cut her off quickly or you'll probably get a rebellious response. Pray about it and tell her what you heard here tonight. Perhaps she'd be willing to talk to me sometime. But be careful. Parents are never aware of how deeply their children can get into the occult."

76

"What did your parents do to you?" she asked.

"Nothing," I answered. "To this day my parents have no idea of the depth of my involvement with Satan and the occult. It's so easy to get trapped. I wasn't even aware of it until it was too late. It's a miracle I'm here!"

At another meeting I talked with a girl who was messed up in numerology — predicting the future through usage of number systems. She told me she now felt she was hurting Jesus through "pseudo-sciences." She tore up her numerology book right there in front of us as tears of joy flowed from her eyes. The Spirit of the Lord was in that room and the meeting lasted until the honking horns of waiting parents forced us to leave.

14

One afternoon in the fall of my sophomore year Gail, a friend from YFC, phoned me to ask, "Roberta, would you like to go with us to Ron's house tonight?"

"What for?"

"Oh, a bunch of kids from other schools are going to be there. Guess it's going to be sort of a pizza party or something."

"Okay, I'll go. Can someone stop by and pick me up?"

"Sure — about seven. See you then."

Ron and Karen Hutchcraft and their baby girl lived in a quaint neighborhood of old homes and tree-shaded sidewalks. The rooms of their small apartment were decorated with antiques they had collected on their travels. It was a cozy, comfortable atmosphere.

When the gossip and eating started to wane, Ron cleared his throat — a sure sign that he had something on his mind.

"I honestly don't know how to tell you kids this," he began. "I'm glad we could get together here tonight." He paused uncertainly.

"Ron," I said seriously, "tell us anything, but don't say you're leaving us."

His eyes widened. "What?"

"Tell us anything, but don't tell us you're leaving us."

He looked away from me dumbfounded. "We haven't told anyone yet, but Karen and I *are* leaving. We'll soon be moving to New York City. I've been asked to be Wayne Area Director in New Jersey." Tears filled all our eyes as Ron began telling us of the new ministry there with YFC that he and Karen felt the Lord wanted them to undertake. Then we prayed together and sang some Christian folk tunes.

As we were leaving one of the girls said jokingly, "Hey, Roberta, I thought you quit all that E.S.P. stuff." I just grinned at her, but I left knowing that the Lord had plans for me as well as for the Hutchcrafts.

I would miss Ron and Karen. We had spent many hours discussing the occult movement among young people and how the Lord might possibly use us to help combat this rising satanic influence.

Ron had told me that the city in the U.S. with the highest occult influence was San Francisco, the headquarters of the First Church of Satan, founded by Anton La Vey.

"Do we have a YFC representative in San Francisco?" I had asked.

"No," he said. "We had a couple of guys move into that area once, but they couldn't handle it. We need someone there who really knows the scene."

"I'm not afraid of San Francisco," I replied. "I think if I ever got the opportunity to go there I could help some of them because of my background. I know how they think. And they do need help. I wish I could go."

Then Ron reminded me that whatever I did with my future, I must always be sure that the Lord was directing and that I obeyed His leading. I began praying that the Lord would lead me to a place where I could help others bound by the powers of Satan.

Now the Hutchcrafts were leaving and I would really miss them — my spiritual parents. About a week before they moved, Ron had me tape my testimony for him. He said that hopefully the tape could be used in YFC clubs throughout the United States, approximately 2500 of them. So the Lord had begun to answer my prayer already. He had provided this method of reaching many who might be mixed up in the occult world.

15

Near the end of my sophomore year, my parents decided to move to my mother's small hometown, Mount Airy, North Carolina — also the hometown of actor Andy Griffith. I was determined to stay in Chicago. Not only did I want to finish my sophomore year at George Washington High School, but I also was very attached to my YFC group and to my singing with "Voices," and I had become a member of a folk group called "The Oblique Future." There was even talk that we might be making a record in the near future. I guess I was pretty stubborn about it for my parents allowed me to remain there and live with my aunt.

However, difficulties soon arose in that situation. My aunt called me a "religious fanatic" and was constantly disagreeing with my Christian views. Her cold attitude caused me to look fervently to Christ for help.

"Go to North Carolina," He said.

At first I cried. I didn't want to leave. There was so much in Chicago that was important to me. But my mother began telling me in her letters that Monty had stopped drinking. *Maybe this is the Lord calling me to help my family,* I thought.

When I told Gene Mastin, our "Voices" director, of my plans to leave, he said, "Listen, if you ever decide to come back to us, consider yourself in the group."

At my last YFC rally in Chicago, I walked through Moody Church with tears in my eyes, trying to capture forever my happy moments there. I hugged my many friends good-by and cried all the way home on the bus.

My stepbrother Joe had decided to go with me, so in June we made the flight together. Our arrival and greeting at the airport was a happy one. As we rode to Mount Airy from the Greensboro airport, I told Mom, Monty, Perry, and Joe about the going-away party my friends from "Voices" had given me. "It was a beach party. We sang Christian songs and people sat around listening to us. It was great!"

My parents had rented a gorgeous house with a fantastic view of the Blue Ridge Mountains. But we were so far out in the country that I had no place to go, no way to go, no one to meet. That summer was one of the worst I had ever lived through. Monty and Joe began drinking together and family arguments flared. My nerves began to bother me and fear again shattered my environment. I was afraid that Monty's drunkenness would kill us all. There was a stable behind the house and I often ran there to escape and pray.

"Oh, Lord, won't they ever change? Please help me." I knew the devil was badgering me again!

Monty came in so drunk one night that my

heart pounded like a hammer. A voice whispered, "Suicide might shake them up." But I discarded that thought knowing it was from the devil. "That is not the Christian answer."

As the arguments grew, my nervousness grew. Then Monty began telling me that I was the cause of his return to alcoholism. I became so depressed that the landlord's wife suggested I see a doctor. "I don't need a doctor. God will heal me."

Finally fall came, school began, and I was able to become involved in outside activities. I visited several churches until I found one that satisfied my spiritual hunger. I began deeper Bible study and had many opportunities to speak, witness, and sing. I felt new progress in my Christian life.

About Christmas time Joey left. I expected Mom and Monty to separate soon, and they did — near the end of my junior year. Mom, Perry, and I stayed with my grandmother for a short time until we found a small house in town. I started working as a waitress at the Blue Ridge Restaurant from 5:30 A.M. until 2:00 P.M.

My long hard summer led into a long hard senior year. I worked part-time after school and spent the evenings drowsily trying to study. As I expected, my grades dropped. But the Lord knew I was doing my best and kept filling my calendar with various speaking and singing engagements.

"Lead me, O Lord, to the next step I must make." He answered my prayer.

Through a letter from Ron Hutchcraft I learned of Nyack College near New York City. It seemed what the Lord wanted for me so I applied and was accepted.

Ron had written to ask about what had happened since I left Chicago. I told him of one recent experience. I had flown to Muskegon, Michigan, for Gospel Films, Inc. to help advise them on a documentary film on occultism which they planned to make. While there, I had an opportunity to testify in their morning devotions. As usual, questions arose and I ran a half-hour overtime.

"I think you gave longer devotions than Billy Graham did when he was here," one of the secretaries told me. I had a rigorous day of interviews there and during that time was asked to read a letter from two girls in California who were Satanists. They were emerging from some bad scenes and the paper told of their initiation into the group. They had had to go to a graveyard in the dead of night, walk across a man-sized cross, and denounce any belief in Christ. Afterwards, a ritual was performed and the girls had to drink the blood of animals that had been skinned alive.

"This is authentic material," I told Mr. Kuhnle, a producer of Gospel Films. His secretary asked me if I would reenact a seance for the film if they asked me.

"I'm not sure. I don't think so. I'd be afraid to," was my answer.

When I left Michigan, I knew the girls would be chosen to make the film for two reasons:

1. They were not yet Christians so the film would have real impact.

2. Their cult sect had given permission to be filmed during a meeting.

Approximately two months later I received a letter from Gospel Films stating that the filming crew had left for the West Coast to work with the two girls. My prayers went with them.

16

Satan still persisted in tempting me with offers of powers beyond my expectations if I would return to my occultic practices. My dreams turned to nightmares as the devil invaded my subconscious. Time after time I awoke screaming, "I believe in the blood of Jesus Christ!"

Strange things began to occur. Sometimes when I was alone in my room the closet doors would rattle. When I tried to determine the cause, I would see a glowering, fiery image which seemed to cackle. Often at night I would be awakened by voices whispering senselessly around me in the dark. I knew Satan had great powers and that he was using them to torment and upset me. He tried to make the good seem evil, to create doubts in my mind.

One rainy evening I had been listening to an album of piano music by Chopin. Shortly after I turned off the music, I went to sleep and began to dream. I found myself sitting before a grand piano surrounded by blackness, and I began to play beautiful melodious chords. Then I noticed a distant ray of light that seemed to come from a doorway, and I soon distinguished the figure of a tall man clad in nineteenth century garb standing in the doorway. I couldn't see his face for it was concealed behind a black cloud, but I sensed that his gaze was directed at me. Then the lanky figure began to walk toward me. As it came around the piano, I rose quickly and backed against a wall. It came up to me, breathing heavily on my neck. I sensed an evil presence and began to shout, "Jesus Christ . . . Jesus Christ . . . the blood of Jesus Christ."

I awoke screaming those words, my heart pounding. A heavy breathing sounded through the darkness of my room. Someone was lying next to me on the bed, breathing heavily! *It's Mom,* I thought. I thrust out my arm to grab her, but it landed flat on the other half of the bed. Yet the impression of weight was there and the breathing continued.

Suddenly I heard a flapping by my feet. I raised my leg in an effort to knock at the thing and again sensed an unearthly presence surrounding me. Then the laughter began.

"Jesus save me," I cried. "I believe in the blood of Christ. In the name of my Savior Jesus Christ I command this spirit to leave me." Immediately the evil presence vanished. I turned on the lamp near my bed and sat up. "Praise God for the blood of Jesus Christ."

My little lamp burned until daylight.

I had read in the Bible that demons shake at the mention of the name of Jesus Christ. *"Why?"* I wondered. I wanted to understand the powers Jesus had left His disciples. One of these powers was *exorcism*—the power of driving out demons.

There are various accounts in the gospels of Jesus using His power to cast out demons, and

90

He said that His disciples could have this same power. I realized that I had been doing this very thing when I called upon the name of Jesus Christ — I had been commanding Satan and his demons to flee from my presence. As a Christian, with the power of Christ within me, I had more power than the devil.

17

In December of my senior year I had a desire to go to New York City. I wanted to visit Nyack College, which would be my future home for four years, and I wanted to see the Hutchcrafts again.

I called Ron and asked about the possibility of my coming up there for a visit. He said that they'd love to have me.

"Flying would be your best bet as far as travel is concerned," Ron told me. I suggested that I come during Christmas vacation, and Ron said that would be great. He added, "If you're here during the holidays, why don't you plan to go to HTC with us (HTC is Holiday Teen Convention, an annual YFC function held during the Christmas holidays with Christian seminars, entertainment, and other activities). This year it's in Niagara Falls, Canada, and I'm presenting a seminar."

"On what?" I asked.

"Guess," he laughed.

Of course — "The occult!"

The only plane reservation that would work out right was on Sunday, December 26 and was an 8:15 A.M. flight, which meant I had to get up at 4:00 A.M. to get to the airport by 7:00 A.M. I would arrive in New York at 9:15 A.M. I made numerous lists of things to take, somehow managing to cram everything into the two new suitcases Mom had given me for Christmas.

Mom didn't feel like driving the seventy-two miles to the airport at 5:00 A.M. in the morning, and I didn't blame her. I arranged for a friend to take me.

I made it to the airport and was soon flying high over the ocean. Seeing the ocean for the first time from that height was fantastic. When we approached New York we hit turbulence and a light rain.

"Ah, the familiar smell of pollution," I laughed to myself as I left the plane.

I went to the baggage area and picked up my luggage and then looked for some postcards in a magazine shop. I paid the man who looked at me with rather propositioning eyes and a whimsical smile. *Yep, this is New York*, I thought.

Ron was supposed to pick me up sometime soon — at least I hoped it would be soon as a couple of hippie-types hollered, "Hey, baby . . ." when I walked past them.

I figured the best procedure was to sit somewhere until Ron found me. By this time my suitcases seemed to weigh a ton as I staggered clumsily toward the lobby. Suddenly I spotted a familiar figure. It had been almost two years since I had seen him and I was afraid to speak for fear it might not be Ron. Then our eyes met, he smiled, and I said, "Gosh, have you lost weight!"

As Ron maneuvered the car out of the jammed airport, he said, "Now, Roberta, hang on. You're gonna see places that you've always heard about. When you leave you'll wake up and wonder, 'Was I really there?' "

He continued, "New Jersey is the most densely populated state in America with a ratio of one out of every twenty Americans living right here. This jungle is the least infiltrated by any types of Christian organizations."

"Are the people rough on you guys for promoting Christ?"

"Naw, just the opposite. These people are so bad off they are literally crying out for help. We have had unbelievable cooperation from businessmen, the schools — everyone."

"Right on! Praise the Lord!"

During our ride to Ron and Karen's home in Wayne we caught up on events of the past two years. When we arrived at the Hutchcraft residence, Karen had a waffle breakfast waiting for us.

"Get plenty of rest today, Roberta," Ron warned. "We've got to be ready to shove off for Niagara Falls in the morning. We'll have to get up at 3:30 A.M."

"Yippee," I groaned.

"We've had to cut out a lot of the formal preliminaries for this convention," Ron continued. "The majority of the kids wouldn't come if they knew they were going to have to attend a hundred different meetings. Most of them are coming just to get away from their parents for three days. These kids are rough and hard."

Later that day the phone rang and I could hear Ron saying, "Okay. That's great."

"That was Tom's mother calling to say he could go tomorrow morning," he said to Karen.

"That's good," Karen said enthusiastically. "I know he wanted to go but his mom seemed a little uncertain."

Ron was scratching his ear. "She said she wanted to be sure the trip was Christ-oriented."

"That sounds good," I said.

"Maybe," he replied. "But she's the head of an Edgar Cayce group."

Three-thirty came awfully early the next morning. Before I knew it, we were boarding the buses, searching for seats. I finally got one in the back right in the midst of a group of guys. Only 7:00 A.M. and already four fellows were passing around a plastic container of liquor. The smell was disgusting. Profanity echoed back and forth and the girls sat in clusters singing dirty songs. I was shocked at the number of girls propositioning guys. Already plans were made to "cop-out" to the guys' rooms once we were in Canada.

Under their breath many were saying, "I ain't going to no meeting about God."

Finally I got tired of hearing it and said, "There are different kinds of meetings. You get your choice. They aren't that bad. I've been before. They're pretty cool."

"I ain't going to one of 'em," a dark-haired boy muttered.

The liquor smell was beginning to make me sick and I opened the window. Soon Ron announced that we were making a brief breakfast stop. As everyone piled out, I sat on the bus and prayed. "Thank God those kids are going

96

to this convention. God has got to be with us."

Gary, one of the boys who was now almost stoned out of his mind, flopped back in the bus with a tray of food. He ate only part of the food. A couple of girls returned laughing and showing what they had stolen from the restaurant. Gary opened the bus window and threw out the dishes one at a time, laughing as they crashed. His buddies tried to calm him down.

"Hey, Gary, watch it. Man, you're gettin' crazy."

"I'll say he is," I remarked disgustedly. "Those people knew you threw that out. They aren't blind. Those dishes are right outside the bus window."

"So what," Gary grinned. "You don't have to pay for them."

"No, but Ron and the other leaders will have to take it out of their own pockets. And they're the ones who'll get chewed out for it."

"You sound like my old lady," he remarked sarcastically.

"Well, I've had to learn my values the hard way. I know your bag 'cause I was in it too. I've gone through the fighting parents, alcoholism, the whole bit, but with Christ I found out I could overcome that hatred. I could cope with my problems and not hurt people."

Gary didn't say another word. Soon the rest of the kids returned and we were on our way again. Some tried to sleep while others continued the dirty songs. We were traveling through upper New York State with its snow-dotted fields when suddenly a pretty dark-haired girl popped up with, "I'm wearing a cross because I've got Jesus and it scares off vampires."

Glenn Dye, a YFC staff member, pointed at me and said, "Then you ought to talk to her — she was a witch."

Not long after that a boy sat down beside me and offered me a cigarette. He introduced himself as Tom.

"No, thanks," I said, "I don't smoke."

He lit one. "Listen, were you really a witch?"

"Yes," I answered. "I was in pretty bad shape. I was a Satanist." For two hours we talked about my life and former powers.

"I believe in Edgar Cayce," he told me. "Have you ever heard of him?"

"Yes, I've read some of his books."

"Well, my mom is the head of a Cayce club. They do some good stuff. You know, like giving Christmas presents to the poor and getting food for people."

"I know, but if you believe in Cayce, that means that you believe in reincarnation. The Bible doesn't teach that."

"This group is pretty good though," Tom continued. "I just get the feeling that they're good people."

"It sounds good," I said, "but I have to believe in the Bible, cover to cover, and I can't believe in something that is not taught by the Lord in the Bible."

Tom was on the defensive. "My mom believes in Jesus. They have prayer and all that stuff."

"Then how come they believe in reincarnation? You've got to believe the whole Bible, not just parts of it. We won't get to heaven because of our works."

Just then Ron came down the aisle and asked Tom if he could change places with him for a few minutes as he needed to talk with me. After Ron sat down, I whispered excitedly, "Ron, that's the guy you told me about who's mixed up in that Cayce group."

"Swell," Ron said. "I'm glad he talked to you. Do you think you made any progress?"

"I think so, but I wish I had a verse to give him concerning reincarnation."

Ron took out his Bible. "Here's one in Hebrews — 9:27 — 'And it is appointed unto men once to die, but after this the judgment.'"

"Good," I said, "that's perfect!"

"Listen, Roberta," Ron continued, "there's no telling how well these seminars will go over. We may not have a big crowd."

I laughed. "How about the opposite?"

"I'm giving three hour-long seminars on the occult, and I want to give you the last five minutes in each to give your testimony."

I agreed to do this, and Ron and I talked for a few more minutes before he returned to his seat. Soon we were going through U.S. and Canadian customs. The boys around me were excited. They planned to hit the nearest Canadian liquor store.

By the time we finally got situated in our rooms, I was beat. After I'd gotten acquainted with the four other girls in the room, I went to bed.

18

Early the next frosty morning I went to the first seminar. About two hundred young people had gathered in the room and that first session on occultism proved successful. We had been right! Occultism was a heavy scene for many of these kids. The number in the second seminar increased. People came to Ron and me asking tons of questions. I gave up my free time to talk to many who had been involved in the occult. Some of them were just learning the beauty of Christ.

At lunch I had a good discussion with some young people who were interested in hearing more about Christ and the occult, and after lunch I met with kids who had been helped to come out of the occult movement and turn on to Jesus through the tape Ron had had me make two years ago. Later I took time alone to visit a museum and talk with the Lord.

"This is fantastic, Lord. Please help me to do Your will."

That evening I had been invited to speak to the Rome-Utica youth group during their rap session. I went into my testimony, answering questions as best I could. The director was ill and asked me to dismiss the group, but said the kids could stay longer if they wanted. Many stayed.

Someone closed the door of the room and we all sat around to talk and share. One fellow said, "They just took Choppy into the next room. I think we ought to pray for him."

"Who's Choppy?" I asked.

"He's a pretty rough guy, messed up real bad. He might make a decision."

We sat in a circle, bowed our heads — some rather nervously—and said some heartfelt prayers for Choppy. I had never heard such devout, meaningful prayers as I heard from these young people. We felt the power of God moving through the atmosphere. Then we heard laughter from the next room.

"Praise the Lord," someone whispered, and others joined in with "Thank You, Jesus." "Hallelujah Jesus." Somehow we knew it had happened. In a few minutes Choppy came into our room.

"I did it." He was so happy. We flocked around him, hugging each other and him and thanking the Lord. What a victorious feeling!

I headed for my room, telling people I saw that Choppy had accepted Christ. I didn't care who I told! A soul had been saved. The angels in heaven were rejoicing and so was I!

On the final morning of the convention I ate breakfast hurriedly in order to get to Ron's last seminar. I wanted to be in the hall a little earlier today. At least I thought I would be early. But when I arrived, I found that the staff members had moved the seminar to a larger hall. When I went to the new meeting place I learned why. Every seat was filled! People were lined up along the walls and many sat on the floor. Some peered into the room and left because of the overcrowding. There were more than three hundred people there for that last meeting. Out of 1,100 teens, more than 800 heard Ron's seminars on the occult. He had been almost without sleep for the past two days, but his presentation that last morning was as fiery and full of zeal as ever. When I gave my testimony at the end, my whole heart poured out and tears ran down my cheeks.

When it was over, a man approached me. "Young lady, you have a magnificent testimony. I could feel the presence of the Holy Spirit move throughout this entire room."

At the final meeting of the rally several young people testified that they had asked Jesus into their lives. Many of them were kids hooked on drugs. I was particularly moved and thankful when one girl cried over her gratitude at being released from witchcraft. The majority of new Christians shed their first heartfelt tears. Choppy was one of them. They were tears of joy because Someone cared. One girl sobbed, "I opened the door and He's just so beautiful."

Before we left Niagara a girl from the Rome-Utica group stopped me.

"You've just got to come back, Roberta. If we took up an offering, would you use it to come back and talk to some girls at our high school? They're really in this stuff bad."

I was deeply touched by her sincere offer. "Of course I'd love to speak at any high school. I'll be going to college near New York so I'll be back." I gave her and several others my address.

The bus ride home was completely different from the one three days earlier. Sleepiness had calmed everyone down. But most of all there was the presence of Christ in these new lives. I got to know several of the kids and then we began to sing of Christ and His love. A small group of girls in the back tried to begin some of their dirty songs, but they soon died out. Victory rang through the bus. Twenty-two new children of God were there — including Gary and Tom.

Once back in Wayne I sniffed a tearful farewell to my new friends.

"Hey, Tom," I said, "I hear you've asked Jesus into your life."

"Yeah," he said, nodding. "I think I understand this better." I told him about Hebrews 9:27.

"Yeah, I know," Tom said. "Ron showed me."

I smiled. "Hallelujah, and good luck. I wonder what your mom will think?"

He grinned. "No tellin'!"

I was flying high for the rest of my four days with Ron and Karen. Not only had I seen many new places and sights, but I had learned so much. Ron helped me find more biblical references against occultism and gave me some new information on it too. The thing which continued to burden my heart, though, was the fact that I had reached only a handful of people who wanted to learn more about Jesus. There were so many still waiting.

19

I have come a long way since that first seance in Dorothy's basement. The more I learn about my wonderful Savior, the more concerned I become for those still trapped and being trapped in the chains of Satan's world.

In speech class during my senior year I often referred to my past, drawing from my own experiences to illustrate "devilish" techniques. My classmates nicknamed me "Witchie-pooh," but I could laugh along with them. No more paranoia!

While in New York with the Hutchcrafts, Ron helped me gather information on proofs of the falseness of various phases of the occult and this has stimulated me to further study on my own. I have many opportunities now to speak and I need good solid material for my presentations.

I remember how I used to wish I could challenge Jeane Dixon, wanting to thwart her powers with my own. I always felt my prophecies were more accurate than hers; she seemed to dwell on generalities, coming to general logical conclusions.

Things are different now. Since Christ has entered my life, I can't challenge her with my psychic powers, but I can challenge her and others with the Word of God which is more powerful than anything else. Through the Scriptures I have learned how to "uncover" a true prophet of God.

"But the prophet, which shall presume to speak a word in my name, which I have not commanded him to speak, or that shall speak in the name of other gods, even that prophet shall die. And if thou say in thine heart, How shall we know the word which the Lord hath not spoken? When a prophet speaketh in the name of the Lord, if the thing *follow not, nor come to pass,* that is the thing which the Lord *hath not* spoken, but the prophet hath spoken it *presumptuously*: thou shalt not be afraid of him" (Deut. 18:20-22).

This is part of the evidence that will uncover the phonies. Ron gave me a list of "prophecies" predicted by many of the popular "public-eye" psychics which have never been fulfilled. For example, Jeane Dixon claimed that the Vietnam War would end in 1965, yet in 1972 it still sizzles.

"Presumptuously spoken," I think.

I have learned that most of the top money-making, public-eye psychics have some record of prophetic inaccuracy.

"I sure wouldn't want to trust someone who is correct only *part* of the time," I say. "Praise Jesus, He is *always* right."

People must be awakened to some of the clever lurings of Satan, as evidenced by the growing interest in the occult which is becoming more widespread every year. Large cities seem to be a fertile breeding ground, reaching the searching young people who wander through

106

them. Young people are especially susceptible to the lure of the occult for they are always seeking answers to life. Many have made a mess of their lives and admit it. They are reaching for an unknown power, some sense of security, just as I was.

People have always had probing minds. Many, whether they believe in God or not, give allegiance to some greater power or being whom they feel is supernatural or superior. Man has a natural curiosity about the unknown, and Satan uses this to trap many into his power.

When a person finds something like a Ouija board or a seance and realizes it is more than a game, he begins to seek more knowledge. And the more he learns, the more attractive the unknown becomes, until he is enmeshed so deeply that he can't escape — except by the power of God.

Satan tricks us into exploring a world over which we have no power. Then he sits back and watches as we go through our rituals, trying to conquer his kingdom instead of turning to God, the supreme Power, who does have all the answers to our questions.

Occultism has even worked its way into rural areas and the smallest towns. In a drugstore in our tiny Mt. Airy I counted between fifty and sixty books dealing with some form of occultism.

Entire families practice witchcraft together. Even some Christian families are becoming involved. While I was in New York, Karen Hutchcraft told me about a devout, happy Christian family she had known when they lived in Chicago. One day the father and son took a flight in their private plane and were reported missing. Search parties were sent out, but the two were never found.

The frantic wife consulted a well-known medium, hoping he could help locate her husband and son, whom she believed were still alive. The medium gave her some latitudinal and longitudinal degrees where he said the plane went down. Again search parties went out, and again the search was futile. By this time the wife and daughter were completely confused, having gone from a strong Christian atmosphere into the satanic world of the supernatural. Satan is powerful!

I still pray for this bewildered woman and her daughter.

The question arises: was it wrong to consult the medium. I believe it was. Our God is great, and He could have used a medium as a tool, but He expects us to lean on *Him* completely — not turn to some other source of knowledge or power. Satan can use these other sources to destroy our faith and stability. The Bible gives us a warning about this very type of thing. "For the time will come when they will not endure sound doctrine; but after their own lusts shall they heap to themselves teachers, having itching ears; and they shall turn away their ears from the truth, and shall be turned unto fables" (2 Tim. 4:3-4).

The interest in the occult is incredible. Recently I was invited to speak to a church youth group where the highest attendance was usually eight or ten people. The night I spoke there were seventy-five present to hear a "former witch" talk about God.

I have been doing careful study of the occult world, seeking out its weaknesses, its appeal, and finding Scripture with which to fight against it.

I can easily spot "surface" cults. I always did believe that any power lay in the "self" and not in outward rites or stimulants. Of course now I know that this "self" is Satan. There are so many who lean on devices such as fancy robes, herbs, charts, books, and other equipment — all weak "cover-ups" for lack of real power. Practitioners of this type seem to admit their powers are not complete. Covens gather together to unite their powers — another example of weakness and belief in old ritualistic traditions.

Astrology is a kind of scapegoat to satisfy an insecure population too ashamed to realize or admit it. These books and seers give only logic, common sense, or general information which might fit anyone at a given time. But people become addicted to this "heavenly guidance." How foolish and illogical to trust a mass of gaseous bodies that cannot think or comprehend life! And yet many people—otherwise intelligent people—live their lives by these human prophets. The Bible says that we cannot serve both God and man — only One can rule our lives satisfactorily.

Recently I have been studying the Edgar Cayce followers more carefully. These disciples have gained a favorable reputation in the public eye. They do good works, make donations for the aged and sick, etc., but again this is a group which trusts in the doctrine of a man rather than the Word of God. Even many Christians believe in Cayce's teachings. They read Cayce more than they read the Bible.

The Cayce books grab the heart with the touching story of his boyhood of deprivation and his great humanity to others. His story gains sympathy in that he was a good man. In reality, Cayce was a deeply religious man, but astounded scientists began putting him in his subconcious state seeking answers about the hereafter, heaven, hell, and reincarnation. Much of it makes sense to the reader, and I can easily see how many are tricked into believing it. I feel sorry for Cayce; he was a "victim of circumstance." He had no control over himself in his trancelike state, and a demon can easily speak through a medium like this.

The pajama parties I attend now are certainly different from the old ones in Chicago. I often explain to the girls about the devil's presence in seances.

"The truth is, it is as easy to obtain a 'spiritual presence with a Ouija board as it is with a seance. The lights are doused and heavy concentration begins under direction of a medium or leader. Darkness sets the mood and psychologically prepares the mind for concentration. Be sensible now. With our knowledge of the devil, we ought to know and do know that he has been here since his temptation of Adam and Eve. He has harassed every being who has ever lived on earth. He knows our strengths and our weak-

nesses. He knows every little 'quirk' we have."
The girls listen quietly. They hardly move.

"Man dies only once. There is no living person who can bring back a spirit. The members of the devil's army recreate themselves and pretend to be the spirit of Aunt Geneva's brother-in-law or whoever you're trying to bring back. Jesus brought back a total man — Lazarus — not just his spirit. Who are we to claim that we can bring back a spirit? Are we claiming that we have powers equal to God's? The devil does anything and everything that will cause us to stray from reading the Bible, from learning Truth. He will try to frighten us into believing. Be on your guard. The problem is that we are so gullible. Remember — 'Be sober, be vigilant; because your adversary the devil, as a roaring lion, walketh about, seeking whom he may devour' (1 Pet. 5:8)."

Some of the girls realize how important Bible study is. We stay up the rest of the night — pure Holy Spirit rapping. If any spirit exists in our presence, it is the welcome Spirit of God.

I have become more and more convinced that parents are responsible to investigate some of the wierd games offered on the market today. My parents never knew the depth of my involvement with my innocent-looking Ouija board. Parents need to keep communication open with their children to know what they are thinking and why, what their needs are and what is bothering them.

Recently I read an account of a young boy who was a member of a Satanist cult. He said

111

he wanted his body to be a sacrifice for the demons of Satan. He begged his friends to help him, so they bound his arms and legs and threw him into a lake. His body was discovered later. His friends were accomplices of Satan — murderers.

My heart is burdened. "Father, I've got to help them. Move me . . . prepare me."

Where will God send me with His message? To New York? To San Francisco? Learning patiently, I watch His will unfold before me.

I see the marks of Satan everywhere. I see his victims. The occult moves on stronger and stronger. The lion roars louder and he must be fed.

I must be a great Lion of God to defeat this lion of Satan. I have found a life worth living and I must tell others.

Epilogue

"In my distress I cried unto the Lord, and he heard me. Deliver my soul, O Lord, from lying lips, and from a deceitful tongue" (Psalm 120: 1-2).

And by grace He did just that—took me from the lying and deceitful grasp of the father of all lies—Satan. Now I pray that I will be able to help people more than I harmed them in the past.

My story doesn't end here, for the love of Jesus is never-ending. My stepfather is just beginning to see the Light of the Lamb, and Mom now realizes that my devotion to Christ is not a fad.

This past summer, after my high school graduation, I spent a few days in Chicago—my first visit there since I moved to Mt. Airy—and Josie and I were reunited. Josie is now a Christian, too, having accepted Christ at a YFC rally under the ministry of Tom Skinner, the well-known black evangelist.

One evening we got together with seven "old buddies" and spent the time talking about the past, present, and future. Several of the girls had experienced demonic appearances or occurrences at some point, and they told me about some of our other school acquaintances who were claiming to be in league with the devil, claiming to be black witches. The number of participants in the black arts had grown considerably since I left Chicago.

When it was time to leave, I said, "As a favor to me, let's all join hands for conversational prayer." In doing so, we thanked the Lord for the beauty of friendship through Christ. Tears were falling—a scene so warm and sincere. Then one friend said, "I don't have Jesus. Please help me so I can find Him."

The prayers began, and we sensed the presence of the Holy Spirit among us. We sensed victory.

"Put on all of God's armor so that you will be able to stand safe against all strategies and tricks of Satan. For we are not fighting against people made of flesh and blood, but against persons without bodies — the evil rulers of the unseen world, those mighty satanic beings and great evil princes of darkness who rule this world; and against huge numbers of wicked spirits in the spirit world."

— Ephesians 6:11-12, *Living Bible*